ACKNOWLEDGEMENTS

I would like to dedicate this work to Imam Ali Ibn Abi Talib (A.S), the Fourth Caliph, successor of The Prophet Muhammad (PBUH) according to the Shia sect. One of his sayings which I would like to share is "Loss is distributed exactly according to the ratio of investment and the profit is distributed according to the agreement of the partners." This is the foundation of the rules of sharing risks and rewards in accordance with Islamic Sharia.

I would like acknowledge the contributions of all who influenced, encouraged and supported me in this endeavor. I would like to recognise the spiritual contribution of my mother Late Mrs. Shirin Ebrahim, who pushed me to pursue excellence, and inspired me to follow the my path to actualise my talents, pursue my dreams, and be the best in whatever I do.

TABLE OF CONTENTS

	Acknowledgements	1
	Table of Contents	2
1	Introduction and setting the scene	3
2	Justification of additional reporting	9
3	Types of Financial Reports	14
4	Conceptual Frameworks by standard setting bodies AAOIFI and IFSB	23
5	Goals of financial reporting of IFI's	29
6	Financial Reporting Challenges of IFI's	37
7	Sharia Governance	48
8	Sharia governance structures	53
9	International Financial Reporting standards	74
10	Future Trends and Conclusion	88
	Bibliography	92
	Glossary	94
	About the Author	98

Chapter 1

Introduction and setting the scene for Financial Reporting of Islamic Financial Institutions

The principal aim of global financial reporting standard-setters is to help general-purpose consumers of financial statements, by giving them the capability to compare the financial performance of public interest entities, to which all financial intermediaries, which mobilize funds from cash surplus units, to be able to provide cash deficient units are. These units would include Islamic Financial Institutions (IFI) and other organizations operating in that niche, on a like-for-like basis with their global counterparts.

As almost all Islamic financial institutions are incorporated with limited liability, and many are quoted on stock exchanges, they are bound to comply with the market regulator's requirement to use International Financial Reporting Standards (IFRS) issued by the International Accounting Standards Board (IASB), which is currently adhered to in116 jurisdictions (early 2016) or the Local Generally Accepted Accounting Principles (GAAP) or supra-national Standard's like AAOFI's Financial Accounting Standards (FAS) or IFSB's standards. This situation usually complicates and confuses global consumers of annual reports and financial statements of Islamic Financial Institutions.

The approach needed would be to develop financial reporting standards, to be used for general purpose financial statements reporting by Islamic financial institutions (IFI). Hence these have to be in sync with globally recognised standards such as IFRSs to ensure consistency in reporting and tailoring them, where appropriate, in order to ensure the financial statements are fairly presenting the balance sheet position, profit, and loss for the period and flow of cash funds of the IFI and can be analyzed and compared with conventional peers, by regulators, securities exchanges and other stakeholders. This approach would increase the credibility and acceptance of Islamic Finance by the global financial community.

Chapter 2

Justification of the need for additional

reporting by Islamic Financial Institutions

The key reason for additional reporting by Islamic Financial Institutions is, because the relationship between Islamic financial institution's and their customers or clients is that their dealing with them differs from the relationships of those who deal with traditional financial entities like commercial banks, insurance companies, various collective investment schemes, and other financial institutions, being a mainly trade based, lease based and equity based, rather than debt based dealings.

As opposed to traditional financial entities Islamic financial institution's are prohibited from the following three elements by the Islamic values and principles:

1. Usury/interest (riba) in their financing and investment dealings;

2. Transactions which involve a high degree of speculation (maisir)

3. High levels of uncertainty (gharar) and;

4. Forbidden from entering into activities that are not allowed by Islamic values and principles.

Example, traditional financial entities mobilize funds and invest these funds on the time value cost of funds (interest), Islamic financial institution's mobilizes funds through investment accounts on the basis of musharaka and mudaraba (i.e. equity-based transaction, with distribution of the resultant gain between the transacting parties in the venture and/or investors who make available the funds and the Islamic financial institution which makes an effort to invests these funds in Sharia friendly assets, contracts, engage in trading activities or leasing activities (ijara).

Furthermore, the information needs of the common users of financial reports of Islamic financial institutions are unique and specific, and, accordingly, the financial reports of such entities must reflect the unique nature of the relationships established with such entities and the transactions, events or conditions involving such entities. These relationships are based on contracts that are equity-based (musharaka/mudharaba), trade based (salaam/murabaha) and lease based (ijara). Qardan hassanah is an interest-free loan.

Chapter 3:

Types of Financial Reports

The financial reports usually expected in the annual financial report of an Islamic Financial Institution would include the following:-

1) Balance sheet showing the financial position at a given date;

(2) Profit and loss account showing the comprehensive income for the period;

(c) A statement that shows the transactions with the owners, and their claims on the business, including profit rate risk reserve and unrestricted investment account risk reserve.

(d) Statement showing the flow of cash and funds inwards and outwards during the period;

(e) Independent Auditors' Report; and

(f) Shariah Audit Committee (Shariah Board Audit) Report on compliance with Shariah Principles.

(g) An account of the inflows and outflows in the Zakat and Sadaqah funds account.

(h) An account of the inward flow and outward flow of funds in the Qardan Hassanah fund.

Sample of Specific Reports in Financial reports of IFI

Sharia Audit Report - Content

- Zakat fund administration

- Sadaqah fund administration

- Reporting on operation of key concepts namely Musharaka, Mudharaba, Ijara, Istisna, Salam

- Reporting of Sharia governance model

- Reporting on compliance with Maqasaid al Sharia.

- Reporting on Non-Compliance noted and. Overall opinion, on Sharia compliance

Specific Funds - Illustrations

1. Zakat Fund $

Balance brought forward	xx
Zakat distributed	(xx)
Zakat for the period	<u>xx</u>
Balance carried forward	<u>x</u>

Narrative description of causes or qualifying institution's to whom Zakat was distributed i.e. only the eight categories allowed and a confirmation, that Zakat was not given to parties prohibited to receive it.

2. Sadakah Fund $

	$
Balance brought forward	xx
Sadaqah distributed	(xx)
Sadaqah from IFI for the period	xx
Sadaqah from contractual penalties	xx
Balance carried forward	x

Narrative description of justified causes or qualifying institution's to whom Sadaqah was distributed, naming the top recipient's and justifying reasons, aligned to Maqasid al Sharia's and Maslah al Sharia..

3. Statement of changes in equity (modified)

NB: Modification is by including 2 additional

columns for URIA* and PRER**

Balance brought forward	xx	xx
Appropriation from P & L	x	x
Utilized during year	(-)	(-)
Balance carried forward	xxx	xxx

*URIAR- UnRestricted Investment Account

Reserve

** PRER - Profit Rate Equalisation Reserve

Key area's where challenges are usually encountered are

1) income recognition especially from equity-type transactions (Musharaka and Mudharaba),

2) valuation of assets and liabilities,

3) disclosure of transactions and presentation of, financial assets and liabilities,

4) valuation, presentation and disclosure of inventories owned by the Islamic Financial Institution from Murabaha (cost-plus sale) contracts and:

5) rights and obligations created from the various modes of Islamic finance, Zakat

(obligatory annual charitable contribution based on net wealth) provisions, sadaqah – voluntary contribution to charity and obligations and rights resulting from some Salaam based transactions.

Chapter 4

Conceptual Frameworks by standard setting bodies AAOIFI and IFSB

Auditing and Accounting for Islamic Financial Institutions (AAOFI) – Conceptual framework

AAOFI has developed a Conceptual Framework that states the aim and the value-based principles underlying the accounting of financial information and reporting thereof by financial entities which claim to adhere to Sharia values and jurisprudence, commonly referred to as Islamic financial institutions ("IFIs"). The aim of financial reporting and accounting by the IFI's to the shareholders, members, and stakeholders is the cornerstone of the Conceptual Framework.

The underlying principles are derived from the concepts, which in turn result in the framework of reporting required by AAOFI for Islamic Financial Institutions.

Why do Islamic IFI's need a set of differentiated Financial Accounting and Reporting standards?

a) To ensure financial institutions including financial intermediaries that use the word "Islamic" in their name or hold themselves out as Islamic sharia-compliant, in their legal aspects and in their commercial substance in transactions, adhere to the values, foundations, and guidance provided by

Islamic laws of jurisprudence in their financial transaction and operating activities.

b) The nature of the bond between Islamic Financial Institutions and their customers with whom they transact differs significantly from the relationship of customers who transact with conventional financial entities, like insurance providers, banks, and other financial organizations. This is because, whereas traditional financial entities mobilize funds and fund businesses and individual anchored on interest, based on time, and amount, but an Islamic financial institution through profit, rent ,and profit and loss sharing. This is because and IFI mobilizes funds via equity-based concepts like Musharaka and Murabaha where investment risk and returns are shared between the provider of capital who avails the bulk of the funds and the Islamic financial institution which avails the effort and some funds and invests these funds in assets or instruments which comply with Islamic sharia using the different types of contracts like musharaka, murabah, ijara, salam, istisna, mudharaba etc.

c) The data and explanatory narrative needs of the consumers of annual finance reports of

IFI's are unique, as the nature of the relationships established with their customers are either equity based, trade based or lease based and involve application of adherence to Islamic commercial law principles, with their unique transactions, events and/or conditions, hence, the annual financial reports of IFI's should reflect these relationships, their effects and affirm adherence to Islamic values and legal regulation.

Chapter 5

Goals of financial reporting and accounting

for IFI's

To determine the rights and obligations of the parties to the transaction, including those rights and obligations consequential from transactions which are incomplete at the reporting date, like advance payment with deferred delivery contracts and cost-plus sale on instalment terms, at a particular point in time, and other contracts like Istisna where the item to be built like a dam, bridge, oil pipeline or highway takes several years.

Hence, for financial statements to be in agreement with Islamic commercial jurisprudence and Islam's fundamental values of fairness, clarity, and adherence

with ethical principles, these financial

statements require additional disclosures, in

the form of reports of accounts.

To make sure the safeguarding of the IFI's

assets, and the informational rights of

interested parties like regulators (central

banks, securities exchanges, tax authorities,

national sharia boards), financial market

participants, and other consumers of financial

reports, when applicable, transparently and

accurately.

To enhance the productive capability,

executive and human capital capabilities of

the IFI and enable its compliance with the set goals and policies and, above all, compliance to the principles of Islamic commercial jurisprudence in all transactions and activities.

To enable the provision, through annual financial reporting, relevant information to consumers of such reports to empower them to make correct decisions regarding their transactions, interactions, and activities with Islamic Financial Institutions.

Information in financial reports by Islamic Financial Institutions

Annual Financial reports have to make available the following types of information:

· Information regarding the Islamic Financial Institution's adherence to the Islamic commercial jurisprudence and its aims and values, to enable the setting up of such compliance mechanism where credible disclosure regarding the method in which forbidden earnings and expenditures, if any, were documented and held after being voluntarily paid in by the parties, into the designated charity account and how these were dealt with, like designated charities to which they are distributed.

Information about the Islamic Financial Institution's,

- assets both tangible and intangible, with their respective obligation of the entity to transfer these cash flows to satisfy the rights of its counterparties or the rights of the counterparties with which it transacts with, and the effects of transactions, resultant balances, other activities and circumstances of the Islamic Financial

Institution, currently available assets and resultant liabilities.

This disclosure should be aimed at assisting the consumer, to adequately evaluate the of the Islamic Financial Institution's capital to absorb losses and business risks; assessing the risk inherent in its investment activities and; assessing the Islamic Financial Institution's liquidity requirements and liquidity position for meeting its financial obligations and its operating requirements in the near future.

- Generate Data adequate to assist in the determination of Zakat responsibilities.

· Disclosures related to the IFI's discharge of its fiduciary duties.

Disclosures related to the IFI's discharge of its communal responsibilities.

Chapter 6

Common Accounting and Financial Reporting Challenges of Islamic Financial Institution's

Asset and liability recognition/ derecognition

Financial assets and liabilities are recognized or derecognized, as and when they fulfill the criteria for the transfer of ownership from customer to the IFI or vis a vis. The variations in those assets and liabilities are recognized when they arise from completed contacts or other activities in a particular period. Derecognition is the elimination of an asset or liability that does not meet the criteria for recognition.

Examples include point when murabaha inventory turn to murabaha receivables (cut-off point), salam deferred receivable recognition, istisna part completed item, with part payment, musharaka and mudharaba profit recognition when accounting period of the investee (customer) and Islamic financial institution are different.

Recognition of revenue

The fundamental issue for the recognition of revenue is that revenues should be recognized when earned.

According to fiqh mualmat (Islamic commercial jurisprudence) revenues should be accounted for in the books as the conditions set out below are met:

a) The Islamic Financial Institution can establish to have deserved the right to earn the revenue, which means that the process through which the right to receive the revenue should have been completed or virtually completed. The exact point at which the transaction's process is complete would change for different contractual financing mechanism, like salam with advance cash, deferred delivery, murabaha on installment sale with cost-plus financing ;

b) An unconditional obligation should have arisen on the part of the customer to pay a fixed or a reasonably determinable sum of money to the Islamic Financial Institution; and

c) The amount of revenue should be known and should be collectible with a practically high degree of certainty, if not already received

Expense recognition

The fundamental tenet for recognition of expense is the occurrence of the event giving rise to the accounting of the expense in that period. This is because the expenditure incurred should be matched to the earning of the revenue recognized during that specific transaction, or it relates to a specified period covered by those financial statements. The expenses recognized that are driven directly like inventory, direct labor, to the earning of revenues, that have been realized and recognized are based on the Islamic concept of attributing the obligation for the cost of the activity or event, to the receiver of the activity or event. Expenses that have no linear connection to revenue like rent, salaries and wages but which, however, have a direct connection to the time period during which the revenues have been recognized fall in two types:

a) Expenses that provide a service to the Islamic financial institution during the current time period, but have no expectation to providing of reasonably identifiable service in the future time period, examples for this include management and staff remuneration and bonuses and other administrative expenses which are difficult to allocate directly to specific tasks performed by others for the Islamic financial institution or identifiable assets created or bought by it. Therefore, these should be recognized in the period when incurred.

b) Costs which are expected accrue value to the IFI, over multiple periods. These costs should be attributed systematically and rationally to the appropriate periods, in which the value will accrue. An example of such costs is the amortization of property, plant, and equipment, which represent an allocation of the usage pattern of the item of property, plant, and equipment over their expected useful lives to the year's that receive the usage value of such items of property, plant, and equipment.

Profits and losses recognition

The recognition of profit or loss, depending on the following:

a) The coming to an end of a mutual or a non-mutual, transfer resulting in the profit or loss. An example of a mutual transfer is the completion of the sale of property, plant, and equipment, and receiving the cash for it, as a basis for the recognition of the profit or loss on the sale of the fixed asset. An example of a non-mutual transfer is the incidence of an event such as a fire, which results in writing off of the item and recognizing the loss on its destruction.

b) The accessibility of adequate acceptable proof reasonably indicating that measurable increase or decrease, in the prices of recognised values of assets or liabilities as a consequence of movement in market conditions. Such profits and losses are estimated unrealized profits and losses arising from the revaluation of assets and liabilities, annually or other periodically, on a fair value basis, as and when appropriate.

Measuring the values

Measuring of the financial impact of completed transactions and the effect of other occurrences during a given time period, in accounting terms this measuring refers to the purpose of identifying the amount at which the assets, liabilities and, in turn, the value attributed to the owners (shareholders and part of the investments of the unrestricted investment account-holders, are recognized in the Islamic financial institution s balance sheet.

Chapter 7

Sharia Governance

Sharia governance structures are fundamental to giving credibility to financial reporting by Islamic Financial Institutions as without these systems there would be unsubstantiated claims that the institution adheres to the value set of Islam and its activities and transactions adhere to Islamic Sharia.

The standard which applies is the Guiding principles of sharia governance issued by the Islamic Financial Services Board (IFSB) in December 2009. The Guiding Principles of Sharia Governance of an IFI are as stated below:-

- Approach of the sharia governance system
- Competence
- Independence
- Confidentiality
- Consistency

The sharia governance structure refers to the set of established structural arrangements through which an Islamic financial institution is able to demonstrate to the global community that there is effective and independent and oversight over matters related to Islamic sharia adherence over each of the following structures and processes:

- Pronouncement of relevant sharia ruling's/resolutions

- Propagation of information to the market participants and regulators, on such sharia rulings and recommendations and to the compliance and operations staff of the Islamic financial institution, who monitor on day-to-day basis compliance with the sharia rulings and resolutions vis-à-vis every level of operations and each transaction.

- Internal sharia adherence review team to confirm that Islamic sharia compliance has been achieved, during which any occurrence of sharia non-compliance will be recorded and reported, and as far as possible, addressed and rectified.

- The annual external sharia compliance audit for independently attesting that the internal sharia adherence review has been properly carried out and its findings have been accordingly noted by the sharia board, and appropriate action taken.

Chapter 8:

Approach to sharia governance structures

In accordance with globally accepted corporate governance standards such as those issued by the Organisation of Economic Cooperation and Development (OECD), IFI's should make informed decisions in their choice Sharia governance structures, so that they suitably maintain the fulfilment of their fiduciary responsivities including that of always acting in good faith, due care, great skill and due diligence towards all their stakeholders. Each Islamic financial institution should be based on its size and, with a view to determining the effect on the number of members upon effective decision-making, decide what size of the sharia board is most appropriate in its peculiar circumstances.

Furthermore, Islamic financial institutions should take into consideration the nature and extent of their operations. And as far as possible, an Islamic financial institution should aim for a Sharia board with a blend of experience (from consultancies, academia, financial institutions) and competencies (finance, Islamic law, Islamic Commercial law, product development etc). The sharia board's could range from a National Sharia Board (where a jurisdiction has one through which all Islamic financial products would be approved and pronouncements issued, an in-house sharia board or using external service providers to be the sharia board.

Competence

The Islamic financial institution should confirm that any individual entrusted with overseeing the Sharia Governance structure meets the satisfactory fit and proper benchmarks. It is common practice for regulatory bodies to ensure that the board of directors and senior management of Islamic financial institution's to comply with certain baseline criteria, in order to make certain the public's has confidence that the Islamic financial institution they are dealing with have employed knowledgeable, authentic, financially capable and who will treat them fairly.

About the importance of the individuals entrusted with overseeing the Sharia Governance Structure as part of the policymaking process of Islamic financial institutions, it is necessary that appropriate "fit and proper" conditions be obligatory on members of the Sharia board. The board of directors of Islamic financial institution may contemplate taking into account the following benchmarks when evaluating the ability to serve, integrity and propriety of persons to serve on the Sharia board:

(i) Character – that is, uprightness, righteousness, impartiality and repute; and

(ii) A person who is proficient and has the right aptitude and attitude, assiduousness, competence, and exercises sound judgment.

We should realise that the above, is not exhaustive and, hence, the board of directors should contemplate all other relevant matters on a case-by-case basis –specifically, characteristics that are appropriate to the market segments that the IFI they are in, and the country's legal and regulatory framework.

In the event that the Islamic financial institution appoints a Sharia advisory consultancy as its Sharia Board, such a consultancy should have appropriate know-how and resources to carry out its work.

A Sharia advisory consultancy should not accept any Sharia audit or review work beyond its capacity and proficiency.

An Islamic financial institution should have the right to check and confirm, from time to time, that the consultancy has the relevant know-how and adequate resources to perform its role properly. The management of the Sharia advisory consultancy should appoint a devoted and experienced team, particularly in the framework of the tasks to be undertaken by the team; and the team should have the personnel and resources to carry out the Sharia audit and review work, to the criterions expected by the Islamic financial institution.

Practically, a Sharia advisory consultancy should be preceived in the same manner and treated to the same rules and regulations related to the use of any other outsourced service providers used by the Islamic financial institution.

Independence

The Sharia board has to play an effective, independent and strong, oversight role, with adequate ability to exercise impartial rulings on Sharia-related matters.

No person or group of people should be permitted to take over the Sharia board's decision-making powers. Therefore, in order to maintain the credibility and integrity of the Sharia board, its members have to not only be able to exercise demonstrate able self-regulating judgement and opinions without the undue, interference, influence or duress, especially from the directors and senior management team of the Islamic financial institution, but also be visible as to be truly independent. In this regard, it would be required for an Islamic financial institution to formalize the independence of the Sharia board and its members by empowering the Sharia board's roles and mandate in its governing articles like the memorandum and articles of association.

Islamic financial institutions should have in place a suitable and open process, like external mediation to resolve any differences of opinion between the board of directors and the Sharia board. This process may be depending on the circumstances, be escalated to having direct access (after duly informing the regulatory authority) to the shareholders as a "whistle-blower" and be accorded the protection usually given to

whistleblowers. The regulatory authorities

may be involved in this process of resolving

differences, without compromising the

binding nature of the pronounced rulings and

resolutions of the Sharia board.

A Sharia board will only be considered

"independent" if none of its members has a

blood or intimate relationship with the

controlling shareholders of Islamic financial

institution, its related companies or its senior

officers that could interfere, or be reasonably

perceived to interfere, with the exercise of

independent judgment in the best interests of the Islamic financial institution by the Sharia board. In the case of Sharia advisory consultancy, they may only be deemed as independent from the Islamic financial institution, if they are not related parties, such as in terms of having common shareholders or common directors.

Confidentiality

The team members must keep any insider information obtained as part of their role in the Sharia Board as confidential. In the enactment of their roles, members of the

Sharia board or Sharia advisory consultancy's, serving an Islamic financial institution could have access to records, operational files, draft memorandums, and conversations that are, under the Islamic financial institution's internal processes and by market practice, are considered confidential. Where a member of the Sharia board or Sharia advisory consultancy, serves many, Islamic financial institutions concurrently, the challenge arises as to how they handle commercially sensitive or confidential information obtained as they are performing their responsibilities. It is a significant concern to professional ethical standards, that commercially sensitive information and or confidential information, obtained by a member of the Sharia board or Sharia advisory consultancy, while serving in an Islamic financial institution must not be used by them in any way that may be detrimental to the Islamic financial institution, especially in a way that could give a competitive advantage to its competitors.

In this context confidential information, refers to information that is received by members of the Sharia board or Sharia advisory consultancy, as part of performing their roles that is not available in the public domain, and not allowed to be made public by the IFI. This normally would include information expressly marked designated by the Islamic financial institution to be kept confidential, given to them under seal, or relating to the consultative processes of the Islamic financial institution. Example of confidential information would be:

(i) Product and or service development information that the Islamic financial institution intends to offer or get involved in;

(ii) deliberations and decisions of the board of directors or senior management; or subject matter of draft opinions or

(iii) memorandum, in a draft or final form, prepared in relation to matters presented, or to be presented, before the Sharia board or Sharia advisory consultancy's;

(iv) the context or rate of conversations among members of the Sharia board concerning matters deliberated on in the meeting of the Sharia board and representatives of the Islamic financial institution;

(v) timing of a decision, or other business transaction, including the status of or progress on a business deal or action not yet completed (except as may be authorised by the board of directors under the internal procedures of the Islamic financial institution);

(vi) opinions expressed by various persons in the course of discussions about a specific matter before the Sharia board; and

(vii) any matter that the Islamic financial institution has designated that it should not be revealed,

such as internal company policies, practices, informal procedures, the content or incidence of statements or conversations, and actions by a fellow member of the Sharia board or Sharia advisory consultancy.

Consistency

The elucidation of the Sharia principles and procedures should be based on the knowledge base of Fiqh al- Muamalat (Islamic commercial jurisprudence) is a usually subject to the expert judgement of the individual members of a Sharia board. Hence, to the extent, the individual who comprise a Sharia board must seek to reach a consensus in reaching at a decision of the board. However, only when a unanimous decision cannot be reached within a decent period of time, should a decision be subjected to majority vote. It should also be noted that st the same time, if the individuals comprising a Sharia board of different Islamic financial institution, should be consistent in the opinions and guidance that they provide in serving on the Sharia boards. Consistency in this regard is connected to independence and competence, as noted above. This is also a matter of professional ethics.

Chapter 9

International Financial Reporting Standards

(IFRS)

The majority of countries where Islamic financial institutions are operating, IFRS compliant annual financial statement are required to be prepared periodically by them, hence annual reports and financial statements of Islamic financial institutions must be IFRS compliant. The conceptual framework of the International Financial Reporting Standards (IFRS) was first issued by the International Accounting Standards Board (IASB) in September 2010 and revised in March 2018. This provides general guidance on IFRS financial statements, including where a specific standard is not available, like for financial statements of IFI's.

This Conceptual Framework for Financial Reporting defines the aims and goals of, and the concepts for, all-purpose, non-specific financial reporting. The objective of the Conceptual Framework is to:

(a) help the International Accounting Standards Board (Board) to develop IFRS Standards (Standards) that are based on consistent concepts;

(b) help the drafters of financial statements to develop consistent accounting policies when no specific standard is applicable to account

for a particular transaction or event, or when

a standard allows a allowed alternative to an

accounting policy; and

(c) help all users to comprehend and

understand the accounting standards.

From the above IFRS are meant for general

purpose financial statements, to assist

financial statements preparers to create

consistent accounting policies, especially

where a specific standard does not apply, like

in case of certain transactions undertaken by

Islamic financial institutions.

A key IFRS that would be applicable to Islamic financial institutions is IFRS 9 Financial Instruments. This is because the contracts under the various modes of Islamic finance, are considered financial instruments.

IFRS 9 Financial Instruments – summary of significant issues

Scope

The Standard would be applicable to all entities to all related to all types of financial instruments.

Impairment

The recognition of the reduction in value requirements of this Standard must be applied to those rights to receive future economic benefits or cash inflows, that IFRS 15 specifies to be accounted for in agreement with this standard for the determinations of accounting for impairment profits or losses.

Initial recognition

An entity will have to account for a financial asset or a financial liability in its balance sheet, when, the entity comes to be a party to the contractual relationship, in accordance with the terms of the instrument. Therefore when an entity initially recognizes a financial asset, it will classify it by following paragraphs 4.1.1–4.1.5 of the standard, and measure it by following paragraphs 5.1.1–5.1.3 of the standard.

When an entity initially, accounts for a financial liability, it will classify it by following paragraphs 4.2.1 and 4.2.2 of the standard and measure it by following paragraph 5.1.1. Of the standard.

Classification

Unless paragraph 4.1.5 of the standard
applies, then an entity would classify financial
assets as subsequently measured at either
the amortized cost, fair value through other
comprehensive income or fair value through
profit or loss. Consistently, applying the same
policy for like transactions or based on both:

(a) the entity's business model, i.e., held for
resale, held to maturity, etc. for managing the
financial assets and

(b) the agreed-upon cash flow characteristics
of the financial asset.

A financial asset may be measured at amortized cost if both of the following conditions are met:

(a) that the financial asset is held within a business model where the goal is to hold financial assets, in order to receive, the agreed upon sums of money, in accordance with the terms of the agreement, future cash flows and

(b) the agreed upon terms of the financial asset produce, on specified dates to cash flows that are solely payments of the principal sum and interest (profit, rent if an IFI) on the principal sum outstanding.

Entities should classify all financial liabilities as subsequently measured at amortized cost, except for:

(a) Financial liabilities at fair value through the profit and loss account. Such liabilities, including those rising from derivative contracts, that are liabilities, will be consequently measured at fair value.

(b) Financial liabilities that relate to a transfer of a financial asset that does not qualify for derecognition or when the continuing involvement approach applies. Then by following paragraphs, 3.2.15 and 3.2.17

apply to the measurement of the financial liabilities.

(c) Financial guarantee agreements. After initial recognition, an issuer of such an agreement shall (unless paragraph 4.2.1(a) or (b) applies) consequently measure it at the higher of:

(i) the value of the loss provision determined by following Section 5.5 and

(ii) the value initially recognized (see paragraph 5.1.1) less, when applicable, the cumulative sums of income recognized in accordance with the principles of IFRS 15.

(d) A commitment to extending a loan at a below-market interest (or profit) rate. An issuer of such an obligation will (unless paragraph 4.2.1(a) applies) consequently measure it at the higher of:

(i) the value of the loss provision determined in agreement with Section 5.5 and

(ii) the value initially recognized (see paragraph 5.1.1 of the standard) less, when applicable, the cumulative amount of income accounted for in agreement with the philosophical basis of IFRS 15.

(e) Contingent payment streams recognized by an acquirer in a business combination transaction, to which IFRS 3 applies. Such

contingent payment streams shall

consequently be measured at fair value with

the movement recognized in profit or loss

account.

Measurement

With the exception of trade receivables (like

those which relate to murabaha contracts),

which fall within the scope of paragraph

5.1.3, at first accounting, an entity will

measure the financial asset or financial

liability at its fair value (agreed by parties at

arms-length), in the case of a financial asset

or financial liability not accounted at fair value through the profit and loss account, transaction expenses that are directly related to the purchase or sale of the financial asset or financial liability.

Chapter 10

Future Trends and Conclusion

In order to that bring transparency, accountability and efficiency to global financial markets, the International Accounting Standards Board which issues IFRS, c, should fast track the development of standards for use by Financial Institutions which claim to adhere to Islamic Principles in their financing and investing transactions. While we understand that the development of Financial Reporting Standards takes time, it should consult with both AAOFI and IFSB to the minimum reporting requirements, these should be content of the sharia audit report, Zakat, and Sadaqah statements, and modified statement of changes in equity to incorporate the unrestricted investment risk and profit equalization accounts.

Financial statements are considered a key communication medium between the operators of Islamic Financial intermediaries and the consuming public of these services, would create give a misleading indication to them if financial statements of Islamic financial institutions, mirror the financial statements of traditional financial institutions, without the additional statements like zakat fund, charitable contribution fund, note to accounts like profit equalisation account,

unrestricted investment risk reserve and

reports like the sharia board and audit report.

References

1. Statement of Financial Accounting No. 1 - Conceptual Framework for Financial Reporting by Islamic Financial Institutions - Accounting and Auditing Organization For Islamic Financial Institutions.

2. Financial Reporting for Islamic Banking Institutions, issued on 2nd February 2018, by Bank Negara, Malaysia.

3. https://www.ifrs.org/issued-standards/list-of-standards/ifrs-9-financial-instruments/

Bibliography

https://www.iasplus.com/en/news/2010/August/news5545 (accessed 24th May 2019)

https://www.investment-and-finance.net/islamic-finance/i/investment-risk-reserve.html https://www.investment-and-finance.net/islamic-finance/p/profit-equalization-reserve.html (accessed 2nd July 2019)

Key standard setting bodies related to accounting and reporting by Islamic Financial Institutions

International Financial Reporting Standard (IFRS), https://www.ifrs.org/

Islamic Financial Services Board (IFSB), **www.ifsb.org**.

Accounting and Auditing Organisation for Islamic financial Institutions (AAOFI) http://aaoifi.com/?lang=en

Glossary

MUSHARAKA

EQUITY BASED PARTNERSHIP SHARING

RISKS AND REWARDS OF A VENTURE

MUDHARBA

EQUITY BASED INVESTMENT

PARTNERSHIP, BETWEEN AN

INVESTMENT MANAGER OR BUSINESS

OPERATOR AND INVESTOR(S)

MURABAHA

COST PLUS FINANCING

SALAAM

DEFERRED DELIVERY SALE (PAYMENT UP FRONT WITH DELIVERY AT A LATER DATE)

IJARA

LEASE BOTH OPERATING & FINANCING.

ZAKAT

A PILLAR OF ISLAM GIVING RISE TO A PERSONAL OBLIGATION OF A FINANCIALLY ABLE MUSLIM AT 2.5% ANNUALLY OF HIS NET WORTH. (SPECIFIC RULES APPLY),

INVESTMENT RISK RESERVE

A RESERVE THAT IS SPECIFICALLY CREATED BY AN ISLAMIC FINANCIAL INSTITUTION TO SET ASIDE A SPECIFIC AMOUNT FROM THE INCOME OF INVESTMENT ACCOUNT HOLDERS, AFTER ALLOCATING THE SHARE OF THE INVESTMENT MANAGER, AS A PRECAUTIONARY BUFFER AGAINST FUTURE LOSSES THAT MIGHT BE INCURRED BY THE INVESTMENT ACCOUNT HOLDERS,

PROFIT EQUALIZATION RESERVE

A _RESERVE_ THAT IS CREATED BY AN ISLAMIC FINANCIAL INSTITUTION BY ALLOCATING A SPECIFIC PERCENTAGE OUT OF THE _MUDARABA INCOME_, BEFORE ALLOCATING THE SHARE DUE TO THE _MUDARIB_. THE IFI BANK AIMS TO MAINTAIN A CERTAIN LEVEL OF RETURN ON INVESTMENT TO THE BENEFIT OF ITS _INVESTMENT ACCOUNT HOLDERS_ AND EQUITY OWNERS, AS A BUFFER TO SUPPORT VARIATIONS IN PROFIT RATES PAYABLE.

QARDAN HASSANAH FUND

THIS REFERS TO A POOL OR FUND THAT HAS BEEN ESTABLISHED BY THE ISLAMIC FINANCIAL INSTITUTION TO PROVIDE LOANS TO THE NEEDY ON THE BASIS OF NO CONSIDERATION OR RETURN. THESE AMOUNTS ARE REPAYABLE BY THE TAKER OF THE LOAN.

About the Author: Mohamed Ebrahim

Currently he is an Audit Partner in Ace Associates –Certified Public Accountants & CEO Ace Financial Advisory Limited. He holds an MBA from **The University of Manchester (UK)** and has worked for over 20 years with firms in Kenya -Ernst & Young – Assurance Advisory Business Service & Tax Service lines, PKF Kenya Audit Senior, and Devani –Devani & Co. United Arab Emirates -Group Financial Controller - Credo Investments FZE. Canada, McTavish & Co.

He served on the Institute of Certified Public Accountants of Kenya (ICPAK) Coast Branch, Executive Council as Secretary and CPD Convener (2013-15) and from May 2016 to May 2018. Vice –Chair May 2018 to date. He was **commended by ICPAK** in June 2015 for his services to the Accounting profession by ICPAK. Furthermore, he has been appointed to serve on the ICPAK Committee of Council, Devolution work stream for the period 2019-2021.

Educational & Professional memberships

Bachelor of Arts (Hons) – Sustainable Performance Management
Manchester Metropolitan University

Master of Business Administration
The University of Manchester – Alliance Manchester Business School

CIFE and Adv. Certified Islamic Finance Executive in Islamic Accounting

Ethica Institute of Islamic Finance, Dubai, UAE.

ACMA,CGMA, Member, Chartered Institute of Management Accountants and Association of International Certified Professional Accountants, registered as a CIMA Member in Practice.

CPA, Practicing member

Institute of Certified Public Accountants of Kenya

FFA/FIPA – Fellow of the Institute of Financial Accountants and Fellow Institute of Public Accountants of Australia

MCSI: Member, Chartered Institute of Securities & Investments

Current Academic studies, a Doctoral Student
   at the Edinburgh Business School, completed
   coursework stage, working on doctoral
   thesis.

QR to ORCID research profile